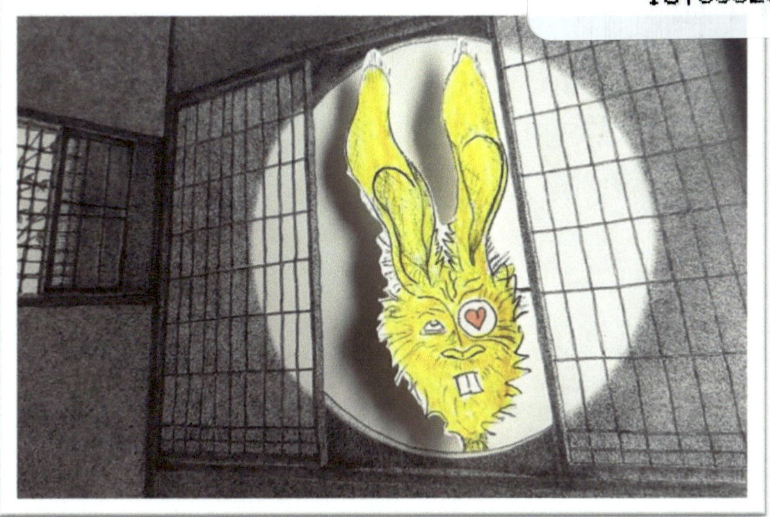

# Stay There

*Japan and Taiwan POEMS*
*VISUAL ART + MORE*


## Michael Klam



GARDEN OAK PRESS
Rainbow, California

*Garden Oak Press*
*1953 Huffstatler St., Suite A*
*Rainbow, CA 92028*

*760 458-2704 (text)*
*760 728-2088 (message)*

*gardenoakpress.com*



*First published by Garden Oak Press on May 15, 2026.*

*ISBN: 979-8-9879532-6-6*

*Printed in the United States of America.*

*to Jennifer and Anya for making loose plans and getting lost with me. . .*

Our father who art in heaven
stay there
and we shall stay here on Earth
which is sometimes so pretty

— Jacques Prévert

# Stay There

*Japan and Taiwan POEMS*
*VISUAL ART + MORE*

Michael Klam

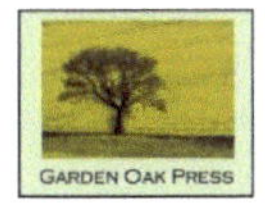

## Contents

### Poetry and Visual Art Made While in Japan and Taiwan

## THE BUDS + *Emma, Anya, Henry*



## HAN'EIYŪ + *Baiguwobo in Black and White*

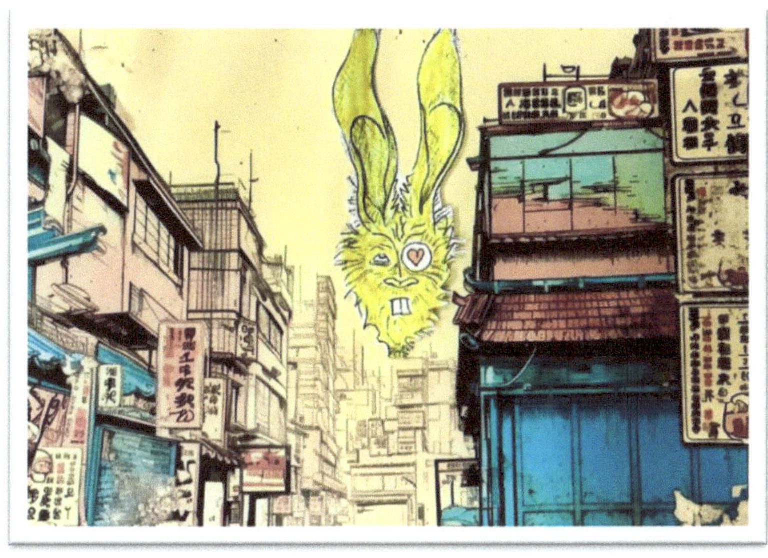

# Poetry and Visual Art Made While in Japan and Taiwan

## Fushimi Inari

Inari is the god of everything.

Whatever is needed. . .
ask Inari.
Pray to Inari.

Especially if you want money.

*Dear Inari,*

*I could die any day now.*
*I got Venmo, PayPal,*
*Cash App…*

*Please help.*

*Fushimi* means:
Underground water.

Fushimi Inari is a mountain cemetery
where tourists and locals visit moss-
covered shrines to take selfies
and pray.

The dead…
everywhere.

Fushimi Inari is a wet, muddy place
earthbound and slippery.

*Dear Inari,*

*I did not fall once*
*in your house.*
*My wife and I…*
*we live in San Diego…*

*It's expensive.*
*We're broke.*

*Please help!*

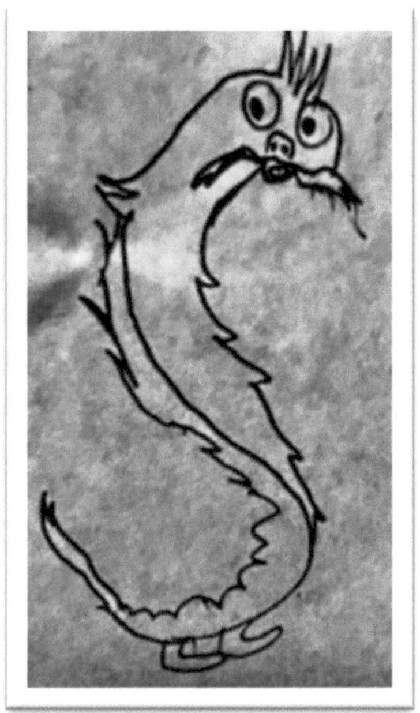

*__Note__: As of the publishing date of this book, the author still has extensive credit card debt.

## Hot Pot Haiku

1.*Oyster Mushroom Hot Pot Haiku*

The oyster mushrooms
in my hot pot have not shrunk
making me wonder

2. *Full Ear Chunk Hot Pot Haiku*

Corn in my hot pot
is full ear chunk that's too big
for my burning mouth

3.*Unsympathetic Chopsticks Hot Pot Haiku*

Enoki mushrooms.
Unsympathetic chopsticks.
Ate you all at once.

4. *No Kiss for a While Hot Pot Haiku*

My wife burned her mouth
on boiled piece of hot pot pork.
No kiss for a while.

## The Art-scientific Mandarin Formula of Us

1)

The variables:

In Chinese, *feng mi* is honey,
*Fēngyǔ* is wind and rain,
and *ai* is love as in the phrase
*Wo ai ni!* (I love you!)

2)

The factors:

In the Klam family. . .

mom is *feng mi*, honey, because
she's an immunity booster

she can soothe a bear

and she's smooth and sweet
and sometimes a little sticky.

Anya is *ai*, love.

Poppa is *fēngyǔ* because
occasionally
he's full of wind
and when poppa cries, the whole world
does not cry with him
but *feng mi* and *ai* grab onto
an imaginary tree anyway
just to make poppa happy like he's
some kind of typhoon made of
thunder and bubbles: *fēngyǔ.*

3)

*Sūgaku* (the math):

Anya, our beautiful daughter, is *ai*, love.

Mom is *feng mi*, honey.

*Anya*
*is*
*ai.*

*Mom*
*is*
*feng mi.*

Anya + mom = honey love.

The Art-scientific Mandarin Formula of Us?

*Fēngyǔ* plus *feng mi* equals *ai*.

Wind and rain
plus honey
equals
love.

## Ishitora Vegan Pit Stop Wrong Choice Haiku

Went on a hunt for
wild monkeys that never came
settled for dry wrap

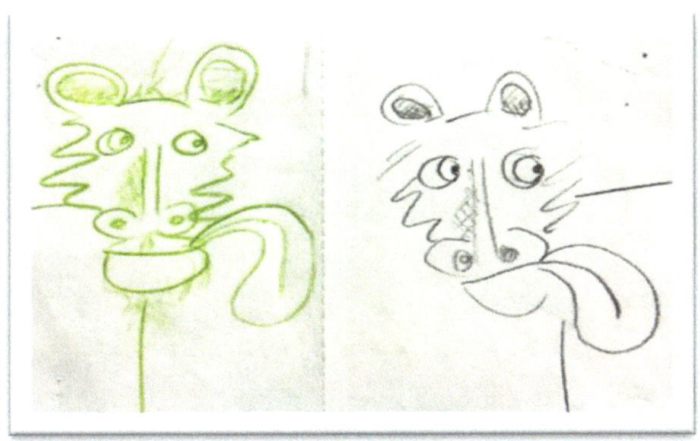

## *Baiguwobo!*
## The Waffling White Devil Superhero

instead of saving the world

*Baiguwobo* gets rejected
by gorgeous servers

in teeny tiny ultra-tasty
trap spots

from Kyoto to Kaohsiung

## Just Another Shooting, Asakusa

When Donald Trump got shot in the ear
on national television, the lives of
his MAGA followers flashed before my eyes.

If the bullet had lodged in his skull
a mere two inches over,
what would have become of his flock?

What would they do now
with no supreme leader to encourage
their overt racism?

Would they have to go back to mostly
seething, their hatred boiling just below
the surface?

I flashed back to that brief moment in time
when Trump's followers on the Right
had to privately tear at their own throats
and suffer through the transgressions of
a liberal stronghold that might, say,
fund public libraries or even support
a woman's right to choose.

We were sitting in a small café
in Asakusa, Tokyo when we saw
on a flat screen TV above the bar
that Trump got shot
and survived.

We must have been trying to get away
from the monstrosity of US politics
because the blood running down his neck
made us feel trapped again.

The owners of the café
and a few local Taito patrons
didn't seem fazed by it.
They spoke little and glanced over
unmoved.

It occurred to me
that this was just another shooting
back at home.

## Hello Tragic Kitty

Lost in Tokyo / in July / sucking on a premium cup of Family Mart ice chips / somewhere in the Kubukicho red light district where / locals eat meat / and tourist parents rage-quest with their tourist children / the $$$ throng stampedes for duty-free Don Quijote and Mickey Mouse deals / & tragic kitty / melancholy pussy is advertised / for sale / everywhere.

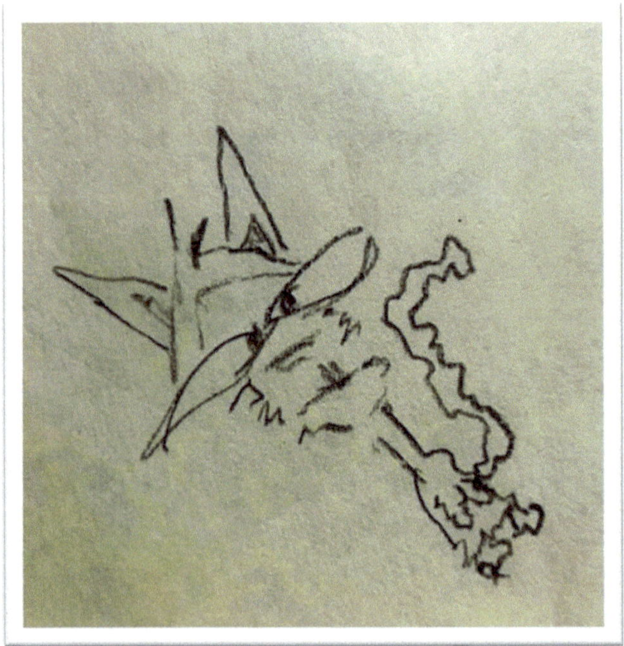

## Xitou Forest Yōkai / No Hello, No Goodbye

She was
all in pink / head to toe
not young / not old
sad silent cold

no hello          no goodbye

suffering the dead
        with us
on the same
        slippery slope down
the same uncertain path this
        dark-green-black-bending
        pathway through
this day-falling forest
        between
the shadows sheathing blades of
fading sunlight again
        and again

she was behind us
        at first
then ahead within eyeshot

if we stopped
        she stopped and stared
        into the trees

if we stood
        she stirred

always alone / never alone
we made our way together
        down bamboo limbo
Yōkai in pink stark contrast

all of us now in pink
to green
to black

she was guiding us
it seemed

only to stop at the end
before exiting the trees

only to stop and stare
into the darkness
into the shadows

as we passed by in perfect
naked
silence

no hello          no goodbye

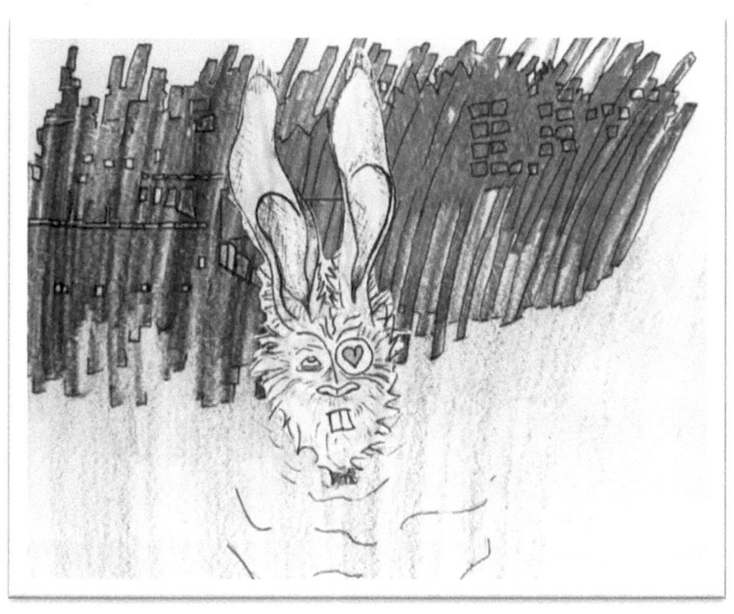

## Hello, My Baby / Hello, My Darlin'
## Plastic Bag Origami Haiku

Made origami
Space Balls alien puppet
out of plastic bag

## Tripper

not one to leave
the addictions
too far behind
I used to
pack up my mind nicely
before traveling

I'd empty the baggies
of course
eat the leftovers. . .
then dry out

unlock, lock, etc.

this way, most of
the suffering
the detox
could be kept
bundled and stored
at home

and the relatives and I
could utterly enjoy
our vacations together. . .

(I don't have to do this
anymore
by the way.

It's great!)

I just have to remember
to pack
the mushroom coffee:

lion's mane for focus
cordyceps for huffing
through the stations
reishi for tolerating humanity

and I must remember to
pack my own pillow
to save my neck

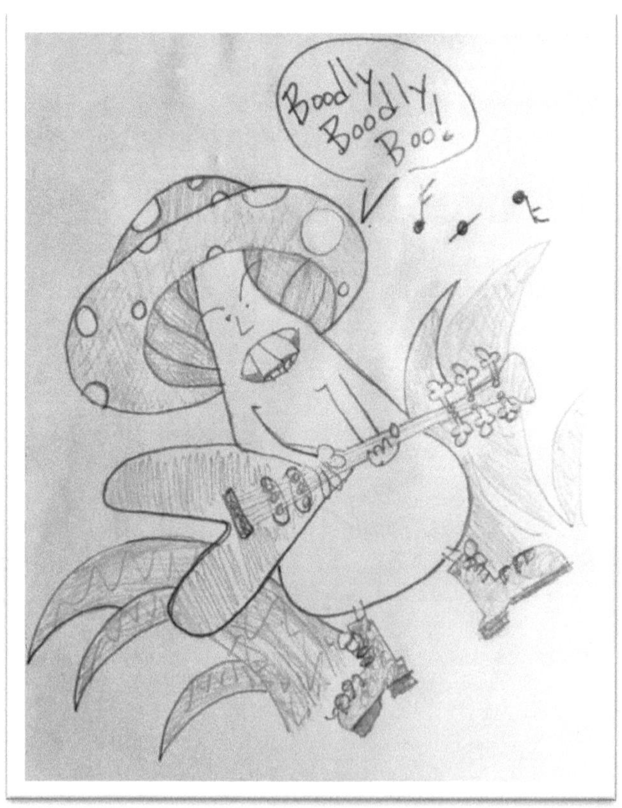

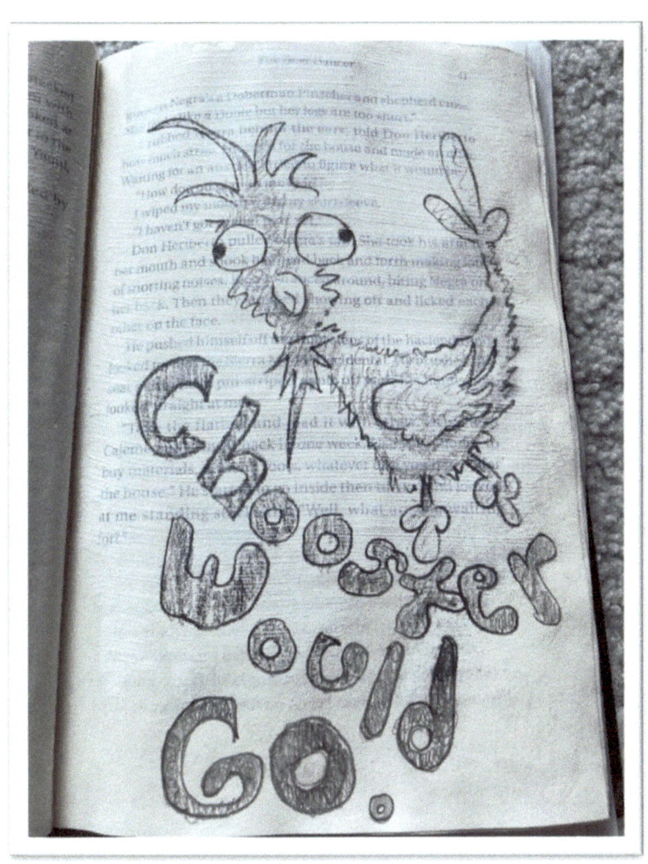

## Japan Rail Voyage: Impossible to Explain Haiku

Missed another stop.
Now racing faster backwards.
Found another train.

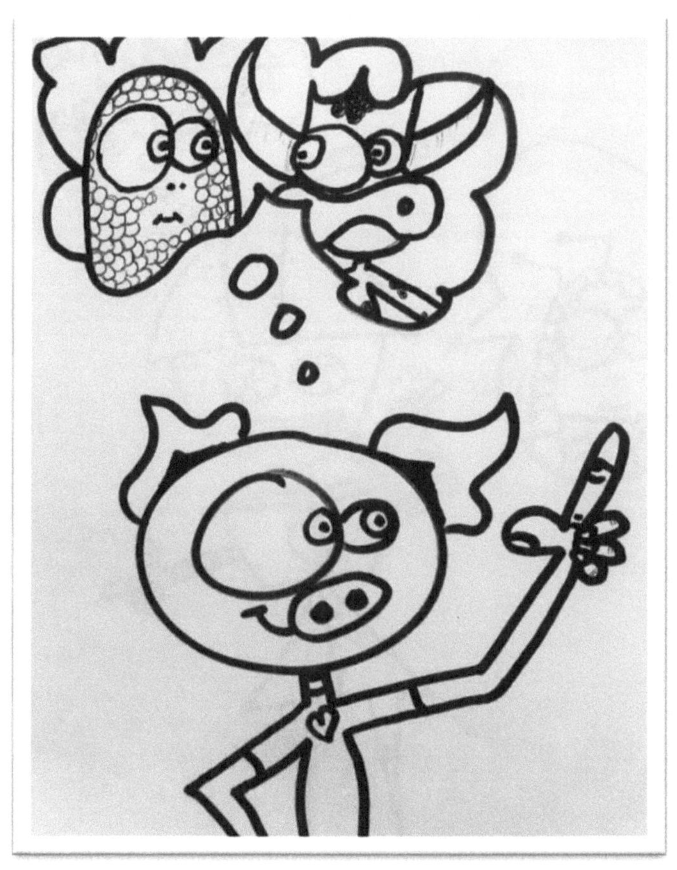

## Thanks, Pam!

sure, some days i wake up to tragedy

an old girlfriend cheating with a lanky
dating game killer whose hair
i don't seem to care much about in the dream
but his hunky presence…
her jiggling enthusiasm. . .

i don't chase the living
i don't chase

i chased once, years ago,
her name was Pam
and i must thank Pam
for having a nice, neutral name
and for teaching me that love
should only be utterly, devastatingly exhausting
when it's real

thanks, Pam!

honestly, in my nightmares, I am, on occasion,
this dreadful pathetic chaser who
isn't fast enough or righteous enough
to catch up and prevail,
get back the girl and kick
all the killer Rodneys' bones to dust
etc.
so, i just pathetically awaken,
the wifey hasn't fled,
and day brings back my snooze button

sometimes, i have this recurring dream that i've
lost my family because i
stopped to look at my phone and
they kept going

i spend the whole dream searching desperately
and feeling certain that they're suffering too
a devout hopelessness
hunting as religiously for me as i am for them
to stop the pain of losing each other

but when i find them
they're just annoyed that i fell behind again
because of my, as they put it, "stupid phone"

it's just awful
i love my phone

many nights, however, i fly feet first,
not like Batman
or a slick, peregrine falcon or a
penguin being chased by a hormonally
deranged teenage orca

i fly in a sitting position
sometimes straight up and down like
in a waiting room or at church, heaven forbid,
but most of the time lounged back a few notches
on the recliner stick, in repose,
enjoying the view as it rushes by

i don't seem to fly in my dreams with any purpose
at all

i never conquer the world in my sleep
but too often
(and once is too often)
a dream will crush me

otherwise, i seem to be on vacation as a dreamer

i drift along in perfect harmony with nothing

i wake up giggling

and for that, dear brain
and dear Pam
i am thankful

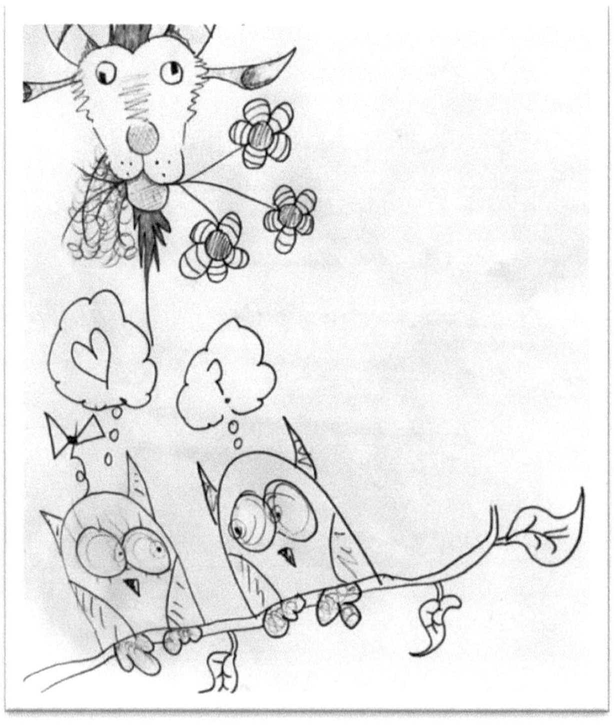

## Sayonara

Goodbye is
a great accomplishment.

It requires saying no
to what you love
or once loved.

Goodbye is a graduation
from yourself.

You hand yourself a degree,
of sorts, and you try to feel proud of
crossing the finish line. . .

Maybe your heart will cheer at times,
maybe like a child, maybe like thunder,
but mostly the faint applause you'll hear. . .

. . .is just time exiting the ceremony.

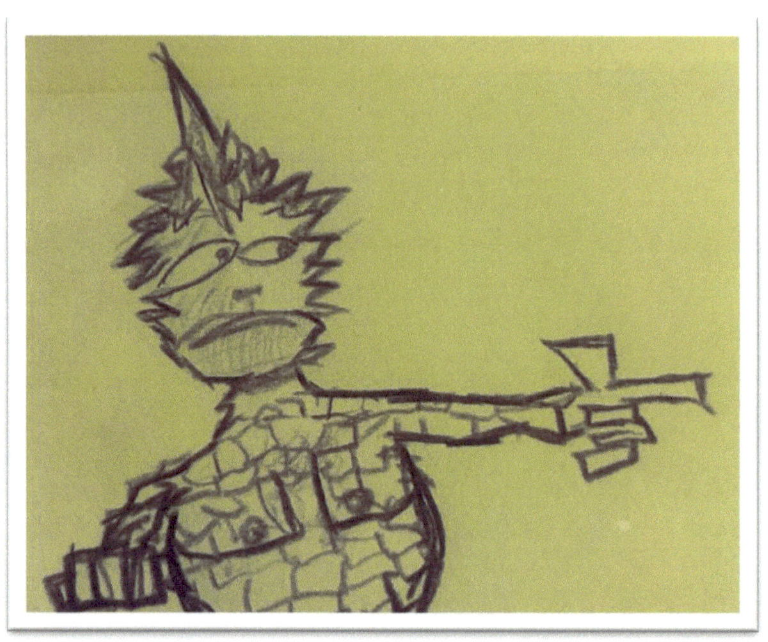

## Faithless Departing, United Flight 803 to Taipei

on take-off
(every time now)
I whisper to myself

*Please crash*

not because I want to die

not because I want
anyone else to suffer

I just think it would be
ironic
to depart this planet
while on vacation

honestly
I'm just as afraid
as everyone else

my whispered
*please crash*
is simply
my way
of throwing *Who cares?*
at the possibilities

I deflect the horror of
the eternity it would take to plunge
from cruising altitude to
the unbreakable glass of
that first sheet of deep ocean

yeah
it's weird…

my *please crash*
isn't 100%

I really don't want to die
I just want to be on vacation forever

*Here Lies Michael Klam*
*Shuffled Off His Mortal Coil*
*on His Way to Do Something Fun*

## East China Sea

Six hundred miles-an-hour
can't sleep
30,000 feet above the sleepless
great whites
and the restless
mermaids
hope and despair
equal and the same

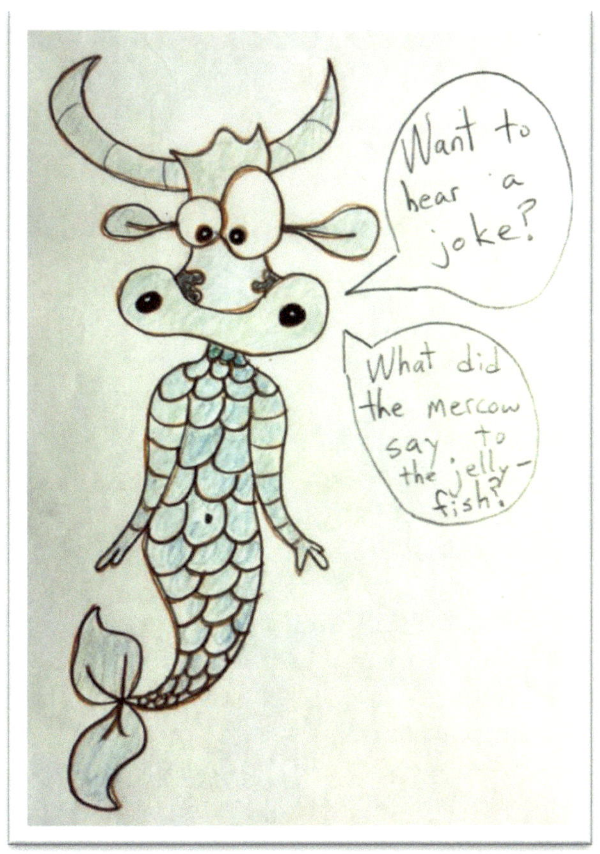

## We made it to Kaohsiung City

Anya's art mind going wild
her journal pages blowing up
the chaos of a single line
the profound nature and order of
a singular dot living in the details

Jennifer's smile
beaming through time
around the sun / over the moon and
back again to get with her family
in the homeland / a promise kept

grandpa Chung up there in years
but his love hasn't aged a single day

I see Jennifer's beauty everywhere
on the island
as far as my eyes can feel
as much as my heart can tell

I'm writing on this trip
dreaming out loud
cracking myself up
because somebody's got to do it
the "happy genius" of the high-speed rail
resolute as it whips over
these elastic landscapes
under this electric sky
all the trains sleek and slick and quiet
the people speaking only in whispers
if they speak at all
a few robotic announcements here and there
unlike home where
the loudspeaker constantly barks
what you can and cannot do
alarm-clocking to oblivion

Taiwan so far has been peaceful
dream-like
beautiful everywhere all at once
and of course

it smells like fish
a lot of fish
and sure, buildings have fallen
and yes, construction accrues
the scaffolding always hungry
for something new

## Two Terminal, Terminal 2 Couples

1)

Soberly navigating her derision
has made him another one of her
dull sailor boys indeed.

2)

Not existing at all
          to him

must be so much more fun
          for her

when she's high
          as a kite

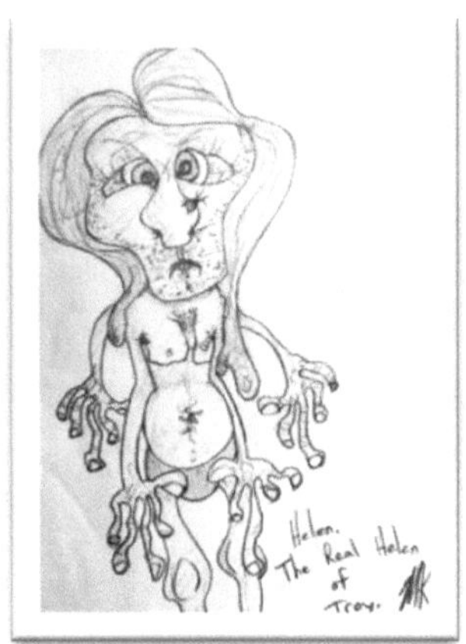


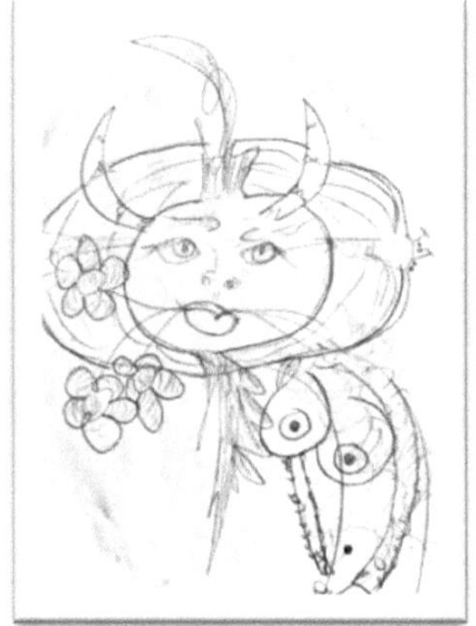

## An Open Letter Poem to the Love Birds Who Don't Feel the Same Way That We Do

Dear dove family in the nest above our porch,

We want you guys to know that we understand the dynamic.

The way that we look at you is not
the same way that you look at us.

Your faces do not say *Yay, they're here again!*
like ours do.

We get it. We should leave you alone. Give you space.
Completely understood!

And if you would be so kind, please consider this:

Stop shitting on our porch. Maybe… fly out a little and
fertilize the lawn?

Warmly,
The Klams

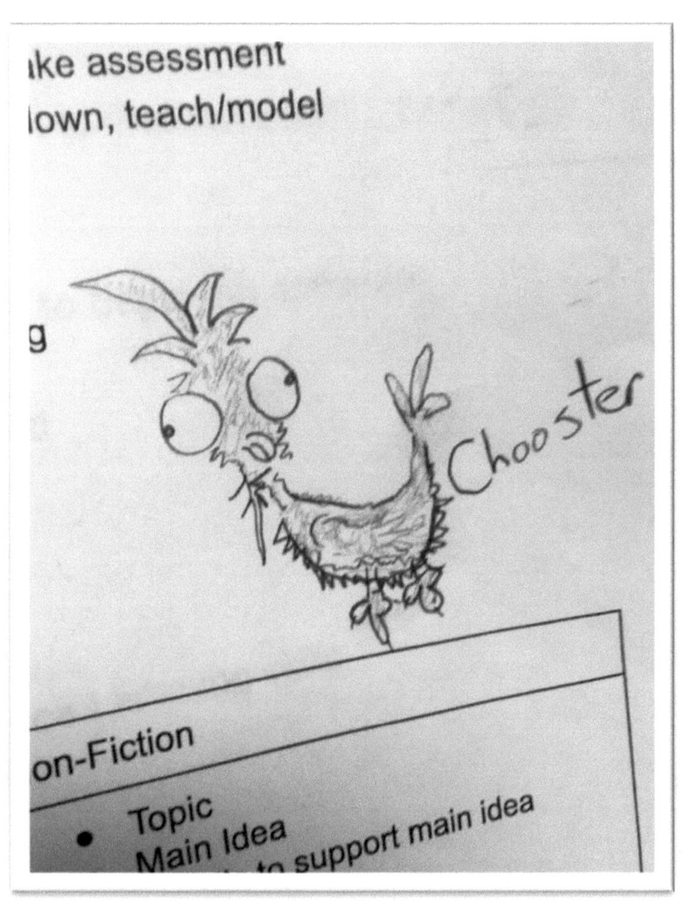
ke assessment
own, teach/model
Chooster
on-Fiction
Topic
Main Idea
support main idea

## One Hero's Banana Peel, Another Villain's Oil Slick

I'm glad I don't have to
fight on top of a train
to be a superhero these days

or fly like a bee or run or even
walk too fast.

I'd hit my head on a pole for sure.

To be honest,
I'm glad I don't have to *save*
anybody. . .

I am. All of you are right:

You can do it yourselves.

I don't even have to be
the villain anymore, really.

It's nice!

Besides, if I got too involved
in your story arc, together,
we would definitely
fall for the old oil trick
or slip on a banana peel
and shatter
our hips. . .

Our monsters would catch us
and eat our sweet giblets.

They would pick their teeth
with our precious bones.

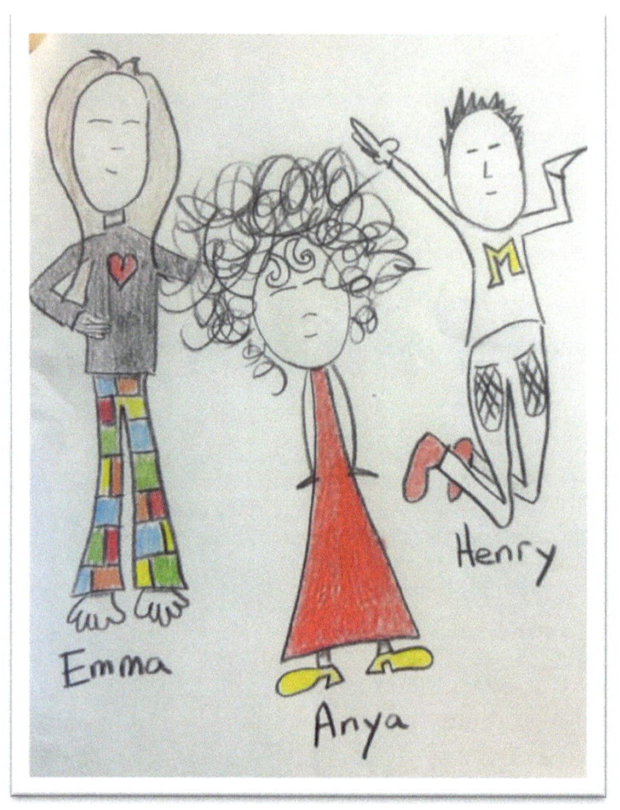


# THE BUDS

## Ta-ku (Taco Haiku): Life Will Fall Apart

Life will fall apart
like a taco at midnight.
Be ready with spoon.

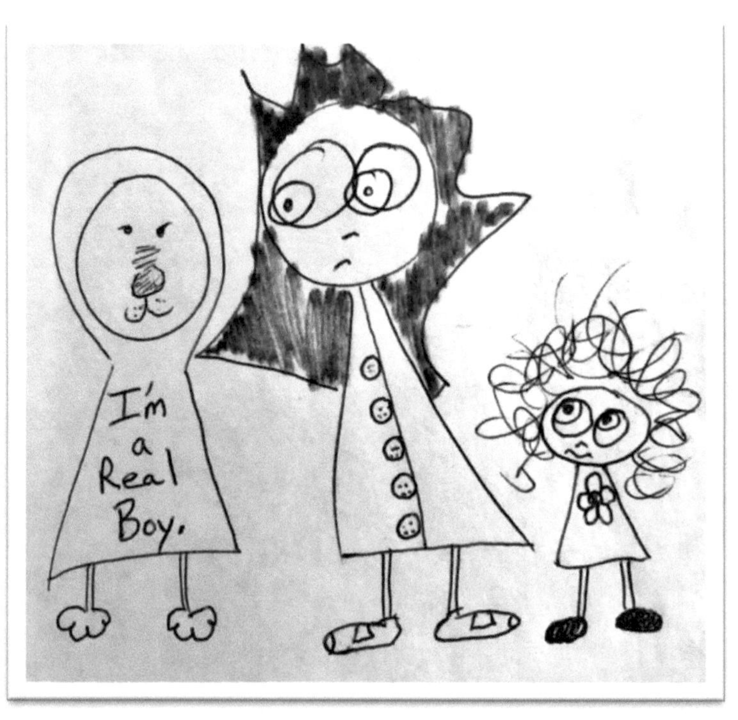
I'm
a
Real
Boy.

## life is wobbly

slip<br>
          and slide<br>
and fall

          like a champion

## Thank You, Smiling Bones

I was 18 and convinced that I had become
the greatest mind of all generations.

I made the decision to visit Grandpa James
to let him know.

I sat on his tombstone above his smiling bones
and I read to him from a journal that I've now kept

in a pile of dust and decaying paper
for the last 39 years.

Grandpa James who mom once said was "loved
like the turf loves the rain."

Grandpa James who knew and was known
by every saint and drunk and priest and stray dog

from here to high water. Grandpa James
who delighted and exasperated Grandma Teresa...

. . .every phrase, every pound, every single penny. . .
Grandma Teresa who once told me,

"I don't drink, and I don't like
people who do." And when I responded,

"But grandma. . .grandpa drank. . ." she laughed and said,
"Well, he'd have his Guinness alright."

I sat there, at 18, on Grandpa's granite headstone
and read my poems so he could hear my epic voice

so he could gather the rest of the dead
by declaring,

"Here's the next poet laureate of the cosmos.
Gather 'round, people! Quiet now! Listen!"

I read boldly to make James proud.
I read to the captivated brethren,

my *daoine*. I read to my hero grandpa
and to the adoring dead.

I read into the ice-cold ether, braying
the trite and terrible poems of my 18th year

as if my hackneyed poetry could resurrect all of Ireland
as if my inane verbiage made any sense at all, I read!

Today, dear grandpa,

four decades after that painful poetry reading,
I've come to apologize to you and your pals,

but I know you won't have it.

There was no excuse. You cheered anyway,
all of you. And you have carried my smiling bones
ever since.

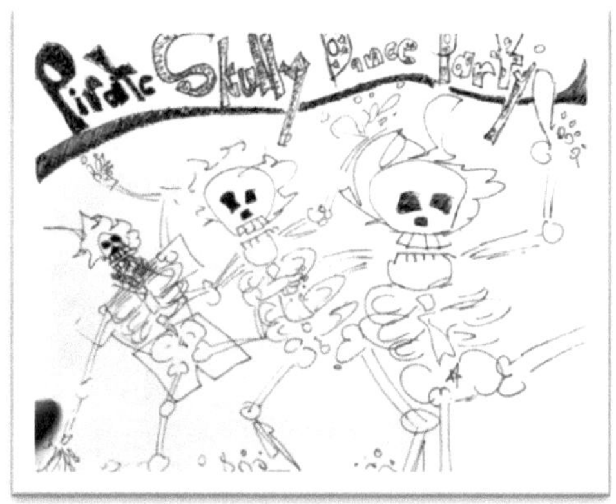

## *Ai* Will Be Home

*a note/poem about your anniversary gift*

*for Jennifer*

So, you might think I
hijacked this book entitled
*Home Poetry*
from one of the Little
Libraries.

I want you to know
that I reciprocated
a *Batman* book in which he
fights a dragon
for some reason
and I do, for all of my
complaining, love poetry half
as much as I love you
which is a lot.

So, take this
and read it
please
because home is where the
heart is (and the mind
according to the strangers
in this book)
and our home is where
your laughter
your words are
(& you're so much better
than all these poets who try
too hard)

not to mention
the love and the snacks

and Anya and Mochi
Emma and Henry
and the baby lizards
the falcons
and Hubie too
keeping a careful watch
on things.

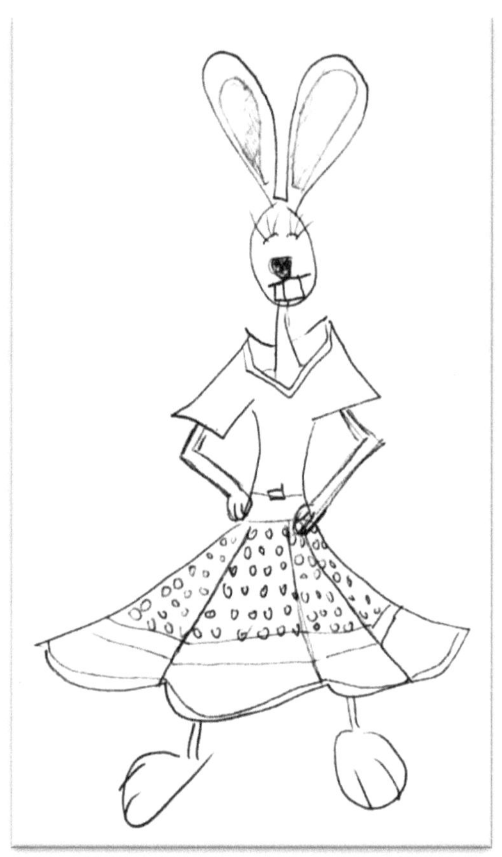

## I Poke You in the Haiku to Wake You Up

I poke you in the
morning so I don't have to
face the day alone

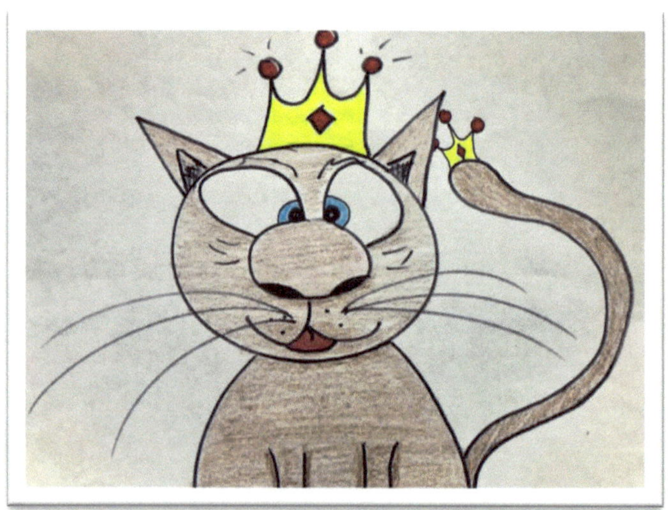

## *Carpe* Poppa

when I hug my family, I say
*Carpe* Poppa not *Carpe Diem*
because I'm awesome
and *Diems* are not always
easy to *Carpe*

when I hug my friends, I say
*Carpe Michael*
because if I said *Carpe Poppa. . .*
that might make things
awkward indeed

when I hug my cat, I say
*Carpe The Guy Who Perfectly*
*Understands You*
because I too can stare at a wall
maybe eat something
fall asleep for hours
in the middle of the day
and wake up fulfilled

when I hug a tree, I say
*Carpe Bibliophilia*
because I love books
and the characters in books
and you who I see
in the characters in the books
and I'm thankful for every page

when I hug the cosmos
I say *Carpe Little Pinkie Toe*
*on the Right Side that I Have Stubbed*
*So Many Times in this Life*
I say *Carpe Digitus Minimus*
and the suffering
makes me laugh

## Out for Summer, Teacher's Take

No more apples
No more bees
No more teachers' dirty knees

Bowww dowwwn. . . Bow dowwwn!

No more scuffs
No more bumps
No more taking Monday's lumps

Huuuuuhh!

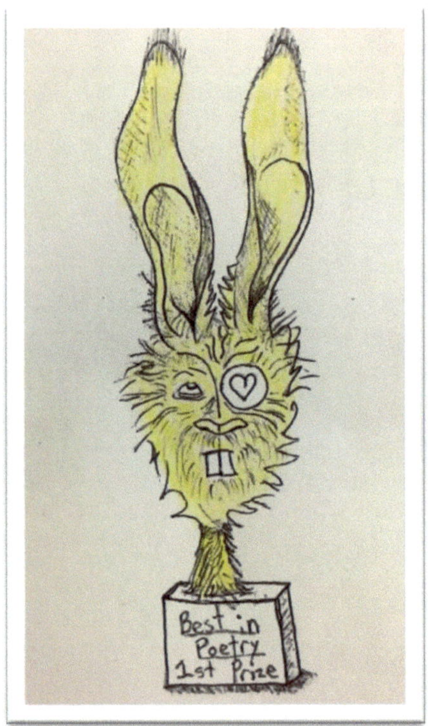

## I Hope You Die Love Poem

I hope you die
peacefully
in your sleep
with me by your side
still loving you
in spite of it all

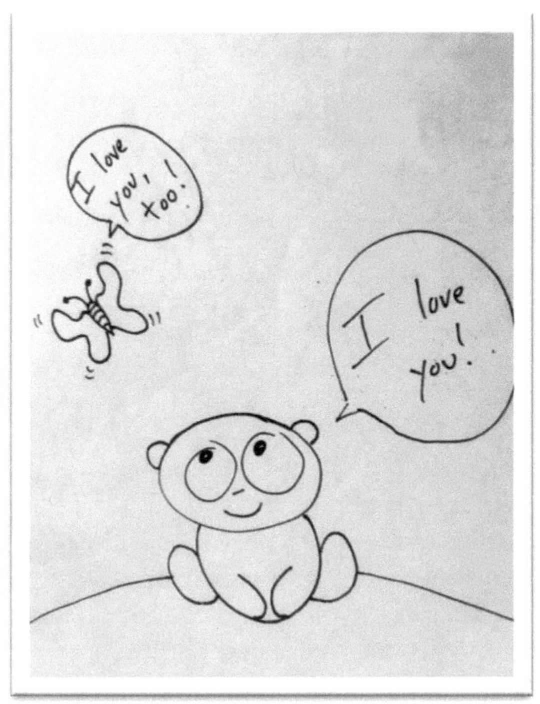

## First Impression, Second Thoughts at Pantages

*in response to Dan Manor's ceramic art,* ***Second Thoughts***

Complete stranger approaches me in line for snacks
during intermission and says out of the blue that he
has a faulty corpus callosum and that the lack of
a stable bridge between the two hemispheres of his brain has
made decision-making very difficult to say the least.

He says his name is Michael (like mine),
and I wonder if maybe we've met before,
but I don't recognize anything about him.

He tells me that as a child his condition
made school tough because teachers thought
he didn't understand the questions. . .but he did. . .
just in too many ways. . . and that in his kaleidoscope mind
even the simplest questions fractured into fractals
of possible answers and second thoughts.

Then, still in line, he stops talking. Awkward silence.
I can tell that it's my turn to speak, but I have no idea
what to say.

So, I ask him what he thinks of the show,
and his eyes lock into what can only be described
as a kind of window to endless paradoxes
and wild loops where answers go to evaporate like
black holes just before they vanish into oblivion.

We quietly stare at each other for what seems an eternity
until he turns and disappears into the intermission crowd.

Left alone, as always, with my thoughts, I realize I should've
said something else, and that I'd spend the rest of my life
wondering if Michael was real or a figment of my imagination.

When I reach the concessions counter, I'm confronted with choices: Coffee or tea, Abba-Zabba, Watchamacallit, Milky Way. . .?

The bell sounds. Last call. I can't decide.

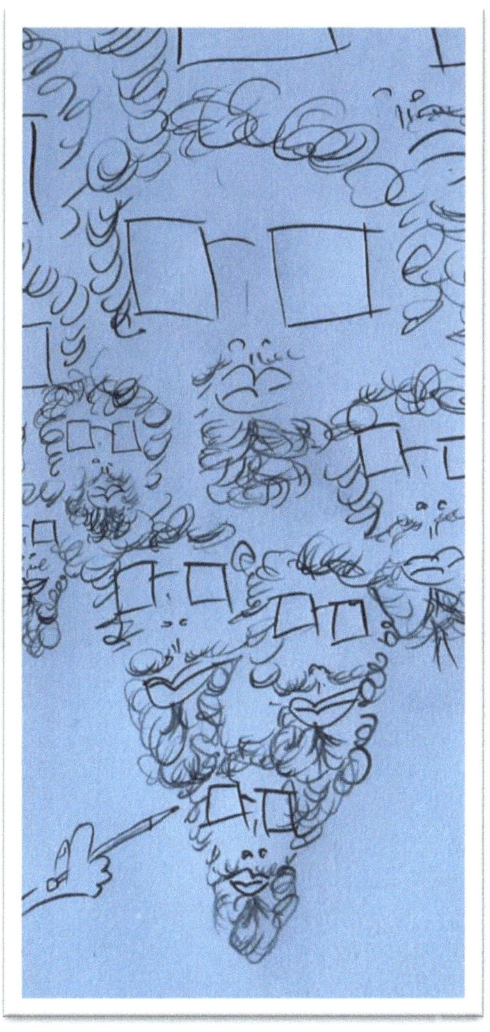

## Find the Exit Strategy

I should feel like
a terrible parent
but often
I don't know how else
to help the children navigate
the same bad choices
that I made at their age
other than to say,

Don't get caught.

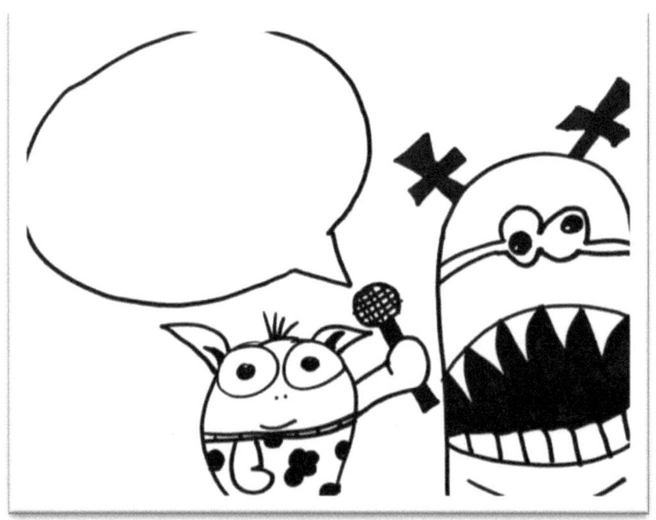

## Career

I was happiest as a teacher
when reinforcing the important things
like how to draw Ponyo

## Marwa's Question

Marwa: Mr. Klam, are you getting old?

Mr. Klam: Yes, Marwa. I'm growing old.
Why do you ask?

Marwa: Because my dad shaved his head
and gray hairs came out and some blood.
He has a pink spot on the top of his head, now.

Mr. Klam: The pink spot is the young part, Marwa.
Everything else,
like the gray hairs and the wrinkles,
is just old skin.

Marwa: No.  He cut himself with the razor.
Old people are clumsy. Do you ever cut yourself,
Mr. Klam?

Mr. Klam: All the time.

## Horse Buds

When I was 16
working construction
in the summer
I was told to dig holes big enough
for 4X4 fence posts
but the soil was gray and unyielding
more like clay.

There were too many rocks, too,
so I had to bend over and scoop them out
after every stab of the shovel.

I dripped sweat.
I cursed the Earth.
I chewed dirt.

I was losing my mind, and the sun
was burning my scalp off
when I felt something blowing
on the back of my neck.

The neighbor's old horse had tip-toed over,
a mare, her head as big as my torso,
her eyes wet and soft like Waneta plums.

She pushed her snout into my chest
and huffed into my belly.

I rubbed her chin and smiled at her
and she smiled back.

Every time I tried to get into the hole
to finish the job, she wouldn't let me.
She'd nibble on my ears
lift me up by the collar.

I realized that she was trying to save me
and that I was supposed to stop and stare
and talk to her.

So, that's what I did for a while
instead of digging holes in the summer
when I was 16.

I whispered that she was beautiful.

Her eyes told me to take it easy.

## Multiverse Schmultiverse!

Woke up by your side.
At home in bed together.
Drifted back to sleep.

## Mochi

many people
I could do without
but it has been an honor
to know Mochi the cat
who chose me

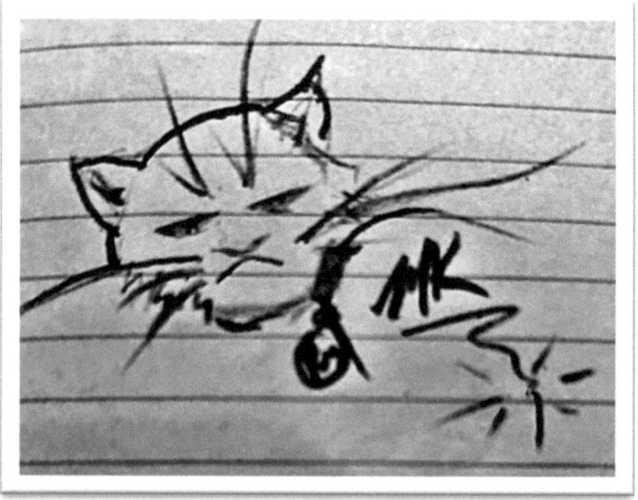

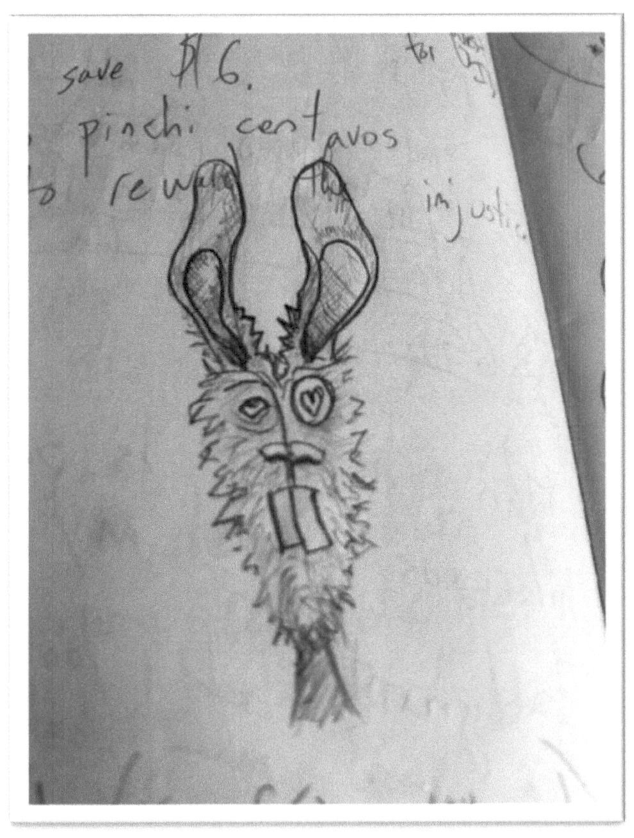


# HAN'EIYŪ

## that's all, don't worry

I have not lost my marbles
they're chipped
they roll funny

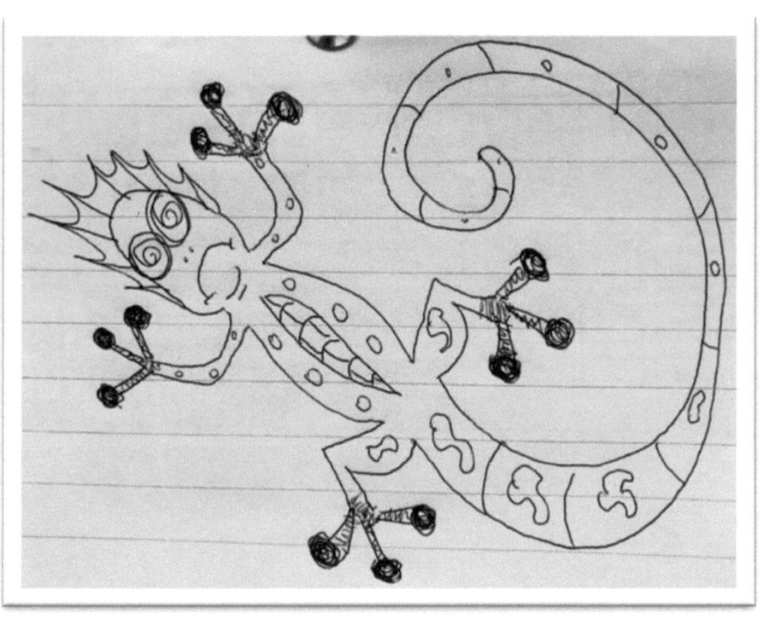

## Depression Poem

sometimes I look at all the cars and think *beautiful*

other times, I think…

*human garbage*
*rolling into the trash heap*

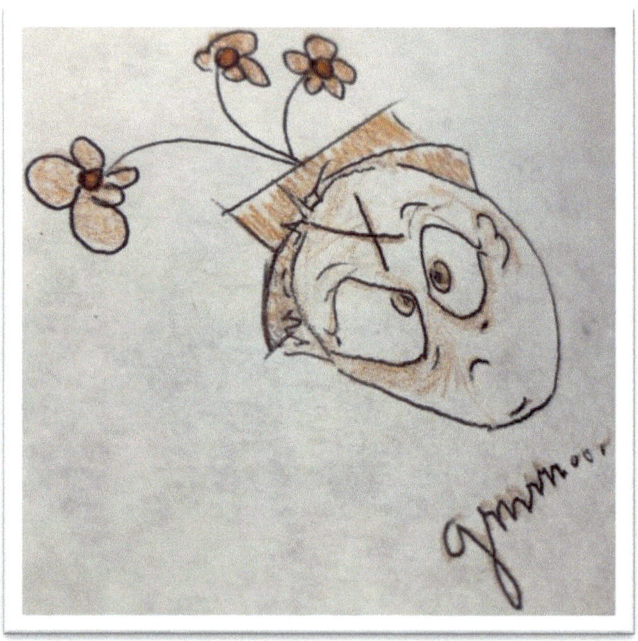

## One Plus One Some Days Equals Zero

On mornings when
adding to the quotient of sorrow becomes
the entire focus of my self-sabotage
should I get on the scale?
should I go back to sleep?
should I try?
should I do my taxes, apply for COBRA,
eat shit, start the day?

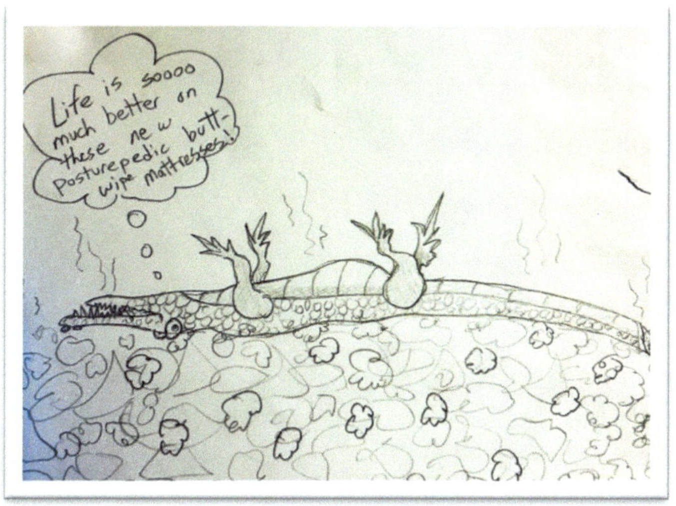

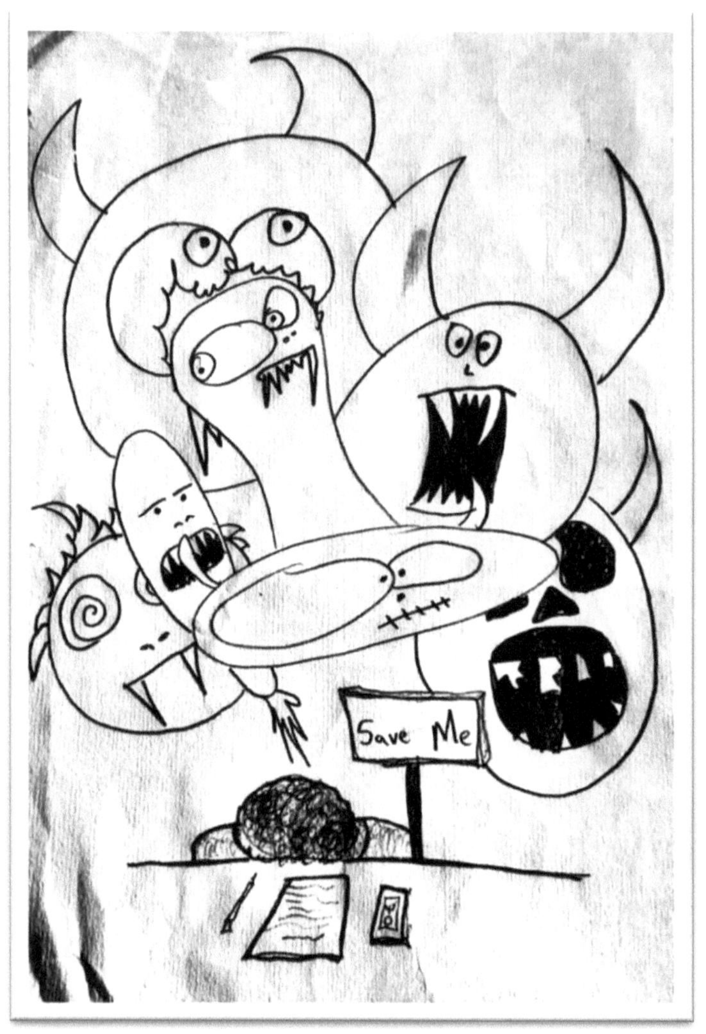
Save Me

## The World According to Mr. H

somewhere a jaguar
rips the guts out of a crocodile
a pit bull saves a child
a bomb tears an irreversible hole
in the history of an entire region

imagine a teacher
in sunny southern california
holding onto an imaginary tree
staring down the barrel of an irate
stay-at-home mom (in the middle of
a custody battle) who has accused
the teacher of being a racist for telling
her dearest child (who is an
absolute mess) to stop disrupting the lessons

"and there's always a clown taking notes
in these meetings, isn't there?
some douchebag clerk who pretends to be
everyone's friend," Mr. H says,

"and a stupid administrator
chewing on her tongue
having another filthy, dry orgasm,
proud of her accomplishments"

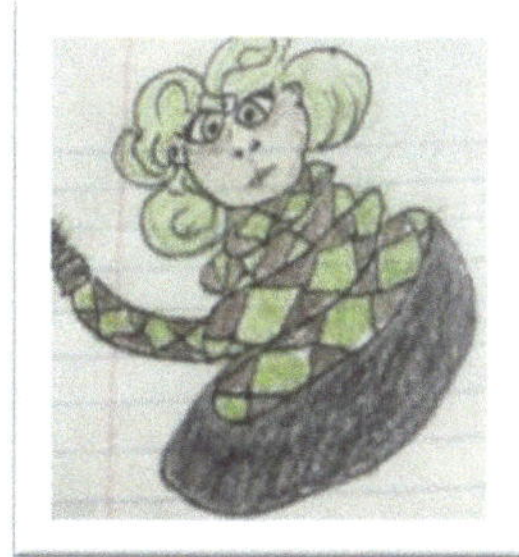

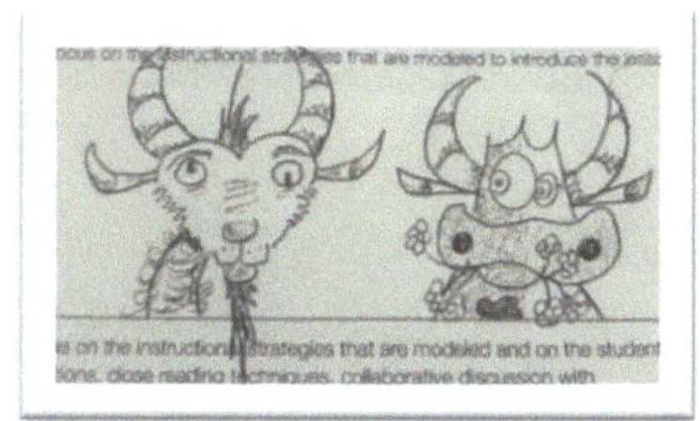

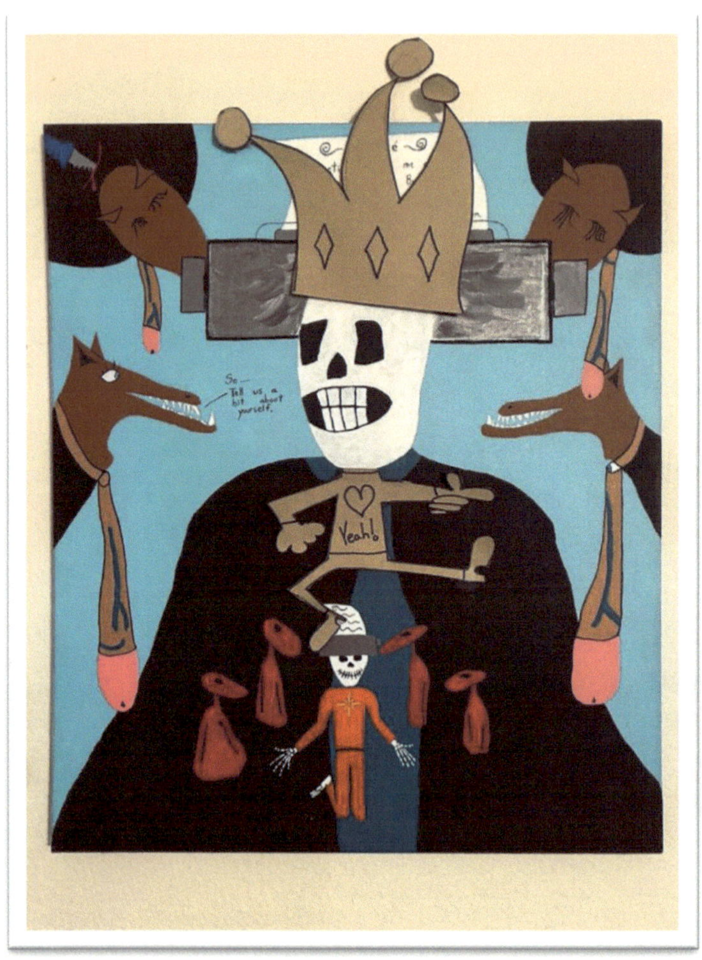
So—
Tell us a bit about yourself.
Yeah!

## PDA

PDA used to be
Public Display of Affection.

Now, PDA is Pathological Demand Avoidance,
co-opted from the autism community to mean
*I can do whatever I want and there's*
*nothing you can do about it.*

We replaced hugging and kissing in public
with honking horns and beating the humanity
out of each other.

*That's my parking spot.*
*I ordered onion rings not fries.*
*What do you mean I can't bring a gun in here?*
*Who's the manager?*

All declarations of war.

When did *Don't Tell Me What to Do*
*Or I Will Kill You* become the opiate of the people?

Or is it the meth?

The hand shakers say, "Don't worry."

Don't reload. Keep scrolling. No need to lift a finger.

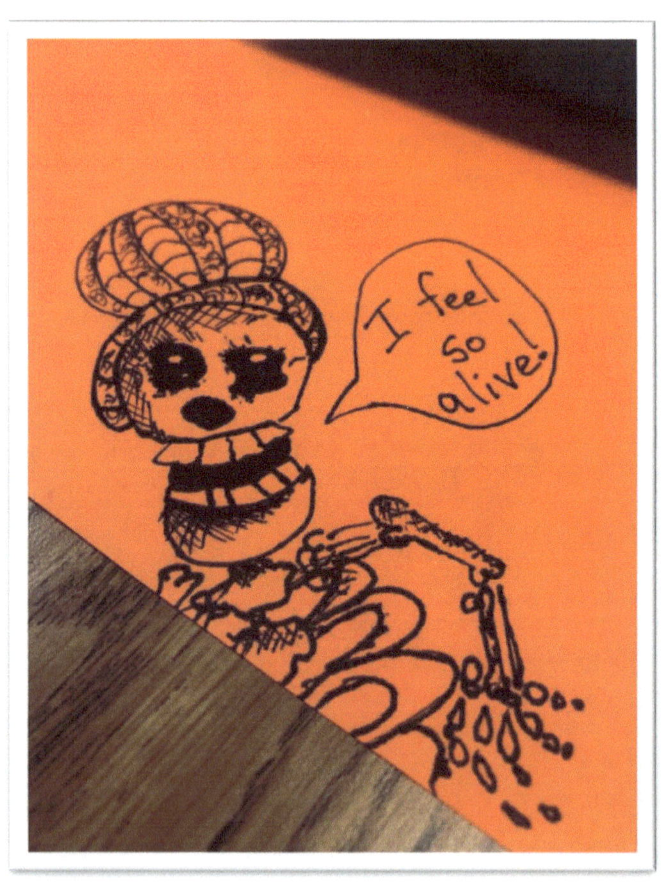
I feel so alive!

## Whispers and Head Kicks and Retirement

Hard night, somewhat
sleepless. Cold.

Whispers and head kicks.
Awake at 2:43.

My stomach
grumbles.

Yet I feel mostly alive,
relieved.

Maybe a little less hatred in my heart.

I'm worried about retirement.

But I earned it.
I need this.
A new chapter.

A shot at grace, a double shot, two fingers
at least.

I would like to remember
how to be in love with the world again.

Shoot. Maybe I'll live longer.

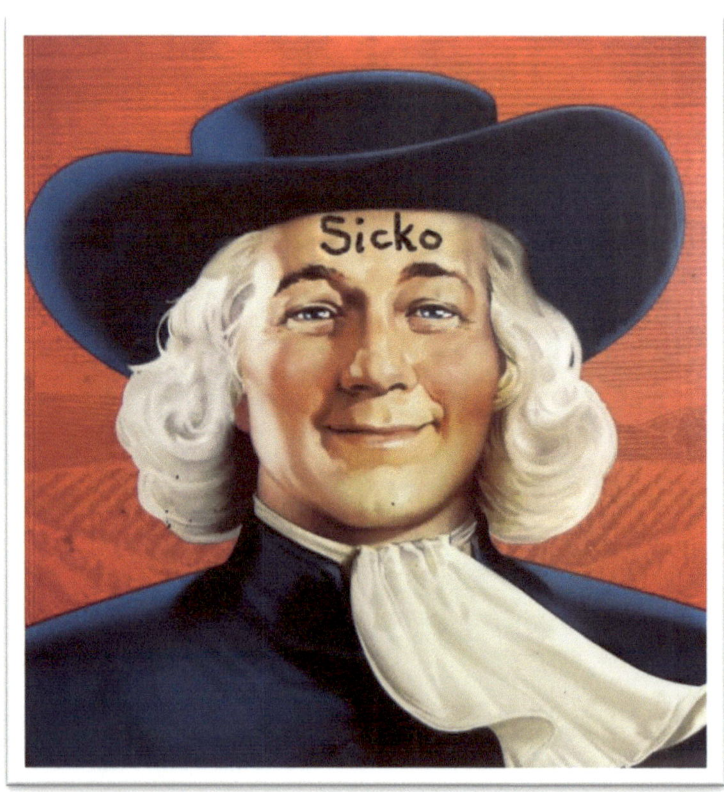
Sicko

## Yoga Despair Haiku

cannot do yoga
cuz the belly is too big
my love wings hate me

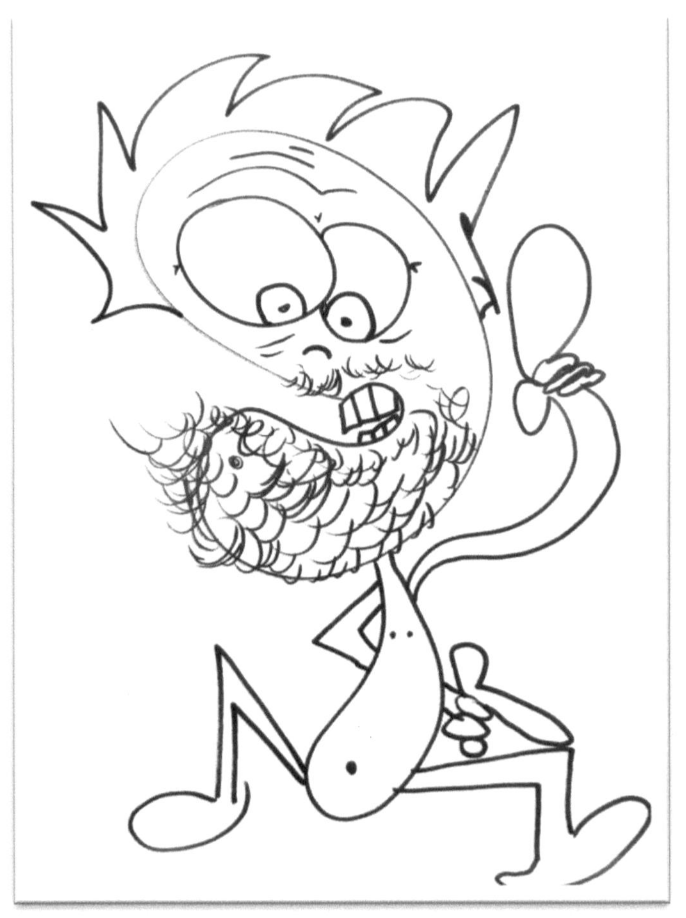

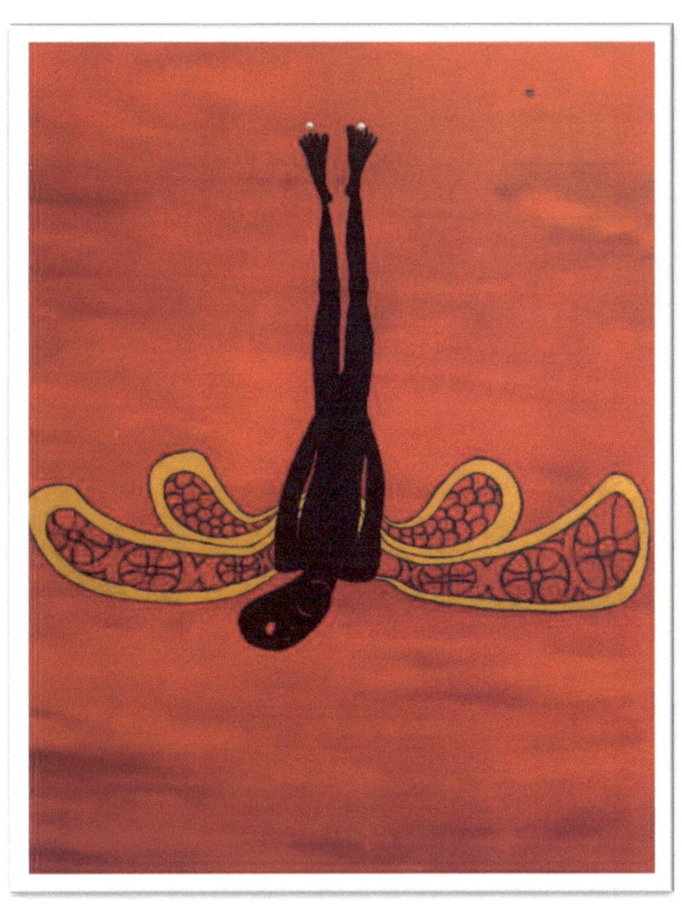

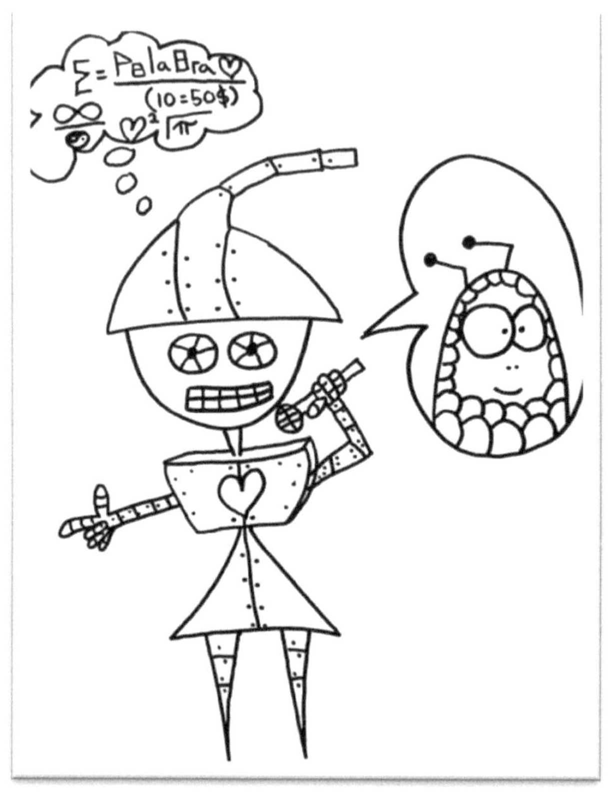


# 7 Poems, 6 Drawings, and a Flier + Poem for Jim Moreno

## Gush

Gush, Definition Number One:

*To flow out*
*in a rapid and plentiful way,*
*often suddenly.*

I am the breakwater built
for your tsunami
the rocks that grip
your pumping shores

the surfer sliding into
swell after swell
of your pulsing lips
your rolling hips
your liquid curls

if waves were poems
I'd be the page that catches
the words that drop
from inspiration
to creation that flows from head
to heart to fingertips
to tongue

Gush. . .

Definition Number Two:

*To speak or write with effusive enthusiasm.*

Your eyes make me gush

Your poet mind makes me gush

Your shoulders, your neck

that galaxy between neck and shoulder
that infinitesimally small yet
seismic sea wave spot
in the middle of your back
makes me gush a gush
that no melting mountain
no quaking earth
no conjuring artist
no storybook goddess
no apocalyptic Neptune
could possibly
unleash

Gush!

Definition Number Three:

*The synonyms overflow. . .*

surge, burst,
spout, spurt,
spill, cascade,
flood, flux,
emanate. . .
enthuse, effuse,
rave, rhapsodize,
wax lyrical. . .
If it were possible. . .

If there could be a one-word poem
to define us. . . it would be

*GUSH*

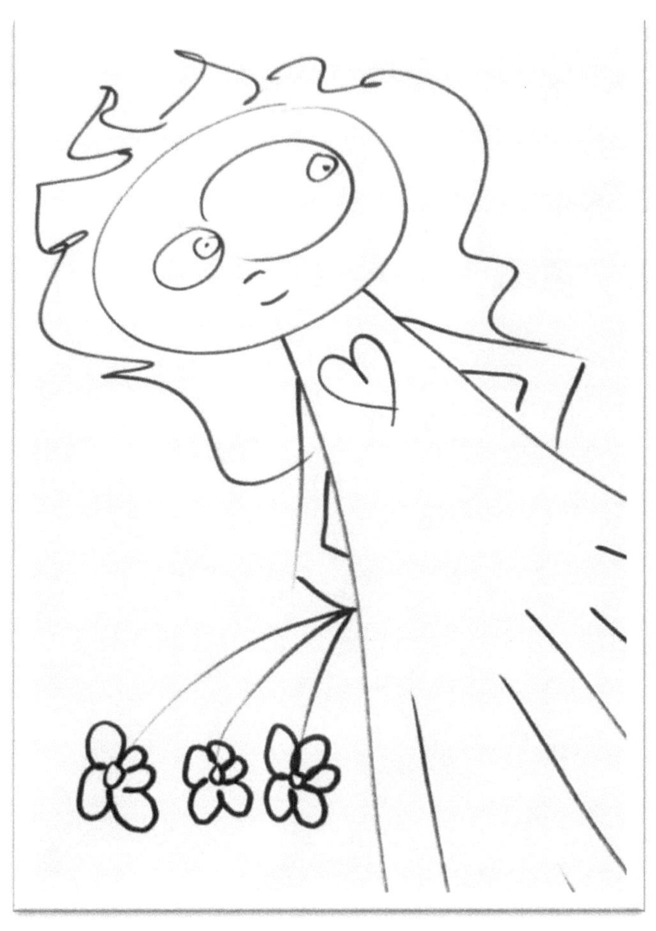

## The Poetry Host Haiku for Robt O

The host of the show
has only two jobs, TWO JOBS!
1) Pacing. 2) Snacks.

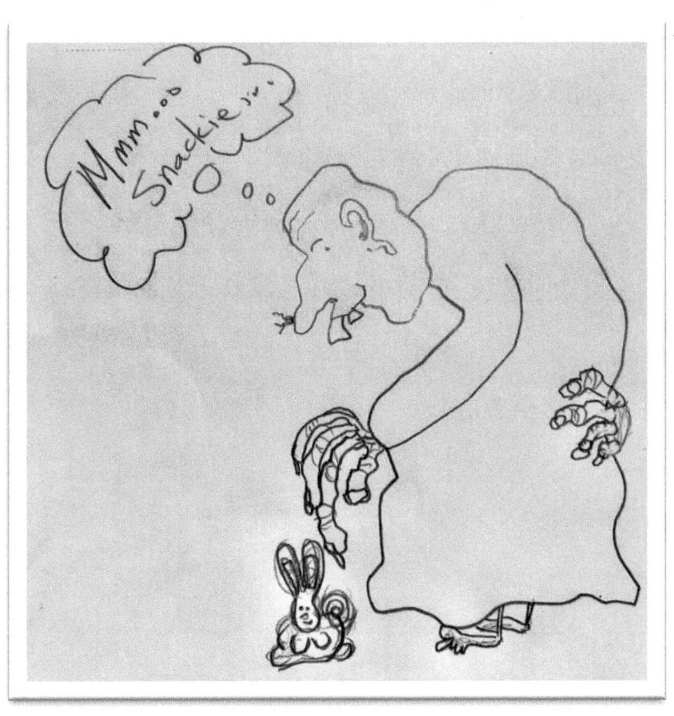
Mmm...
Snackie...

## Serial Killer Husband Material

My wife says I looked like a
serial killer when we first met.

I must've been pretty fucking charming
considering how squeamish I am

when it comes to pain and suffering.

## Gravity Draws Me Like One of Its French Girls

*San Francisco, Summer, 2023*

#1 *Aging Gracefully*

I moan every time I sit down now.
It's just a thing. I'm 54. Is that old?

Gravity plays me like an accordion.
It takes hold of the space-time curvature
of my gluteus maximus and squeezes me
into the seat or down on my knees
and that is precisely when
an inharmonious groan
a kind of pleasureless music of the spheres
blows through my lips.

#2 *Busking Dad's Boy at Bus Stop Explains My Situation*

Fulton and La Playa
as far west as possible
with Anya, 12, and Jennifer, not much
younger than me but gorgeous,
waiting for SF Mun. Bus #44.

I moan when I sit down next to a boy
and his dad and a guitar.

"I think you are very old, right?" says the boy
who is so skinny and so frail he would seem dead
if it weren't for his innocuous smile.

I like him instantaneously, so I tell him
*Yes, I've been old for a very long time.*

His dad eats cranberries and looks out at
the hungry street. The guitar is quiet. It's
cold by the ocean.

"You can't stand up forever when you're old,"
his son reminds me.

"Well," his dad clarifies, "Nobody can stand up
forever."

We all agree.

#3 *Bearded Teenager Ferris Wheel Attendant at Golden*
*Gate Park Asks Me if I'm 65+*

For some reason this moment is particularly
hilarious to Anya and Jennifer.

Again, *I'm only 54!*

I notice on the price board that there's no
other option after 65+. There is no 70+, for example!

Indignant, I look at the wee man behind the glass,
right into in his cold, dead eyes and lie to him,
*Yes, I am over 65.*

He doesn't blink a wrinkle-free lid.
No questions asked. No request for ID.

I save the family $6. Six hundred *pinchi centavos*
to reward the injustice.

I'm puzzled and guessing that this is the discount era,
the beginning of the end, when Anya leans in and
joke-whispers, "For 65+, you look great, Poppa."

## Gustavo

They say he used to be a narco. . .
but who knows?

Gustavo looks like a botanist to me.
Maybe a florist.

Or a mechanical engineer?

## well then

the birds and the bubbles
the chalk and the cheese

it's all the same / stiff wind cool breeze
a diamond in a drop of antifreeze

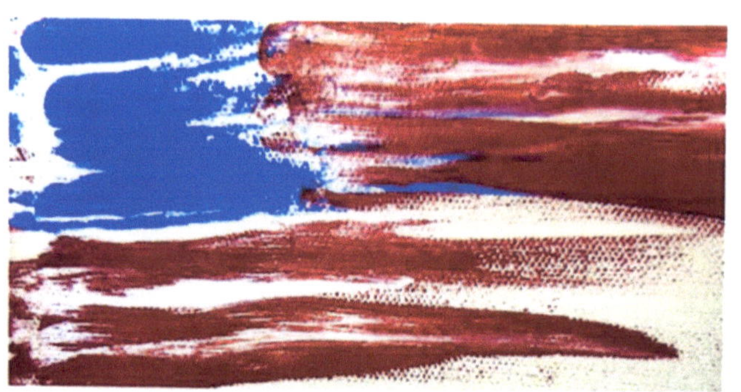

**SAN DIEGO POETRY ANNUAL – VETERANS CELEBRATION AND COMMUNITY OPEN MIC**

Hosted by Veterans/SDPA editors
Billiekai Boughton and Jim Moreno

**June 29 @ 3:00 pm**
**San Diego Writers, Ink**
**2730 Historic Decatur Road #204**
**Liberty Station**

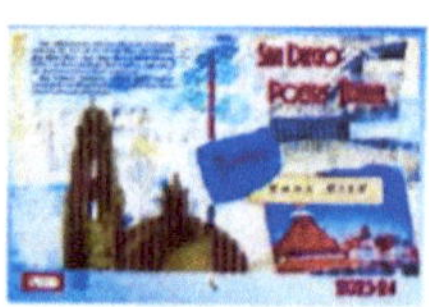

Veterans published in the 2023-24 SDPA will be honored and invited to read first. All military and friends and families of military welcome to share on the open mic following the features. Open to the general public.

Details and signups: @billiekaiboughton and @sdpoetryannual

## Walking Meditation

*for Jim*

I went to Sunset Cliffs today
to see the spring flowers.

Ten teenage boys
came out of the canyon
with paintball guns.

They had just played war.

One of them shot a metal sign that said
DANGEROUS CLIFFS STAY BACK
and he left a splatter of silver paint
over the word *DANGEROUS*.

Two of the boys shot the ground.
I imagine they were trying to *kill*
the ground.

Another fired into the *Eucalyptus*.

How easy it seems for boys to become
warriors and to be war.

Being peace, on the other hand,
requires deeper thinking.

Today in the Sunset Cliffs Natural Park
the early flowers of spring defied the ugliness
of a nation bred on violence

and although there was a genuine lack
of human thought and contemplation in the air

peace whispered its beauty
through the trees.

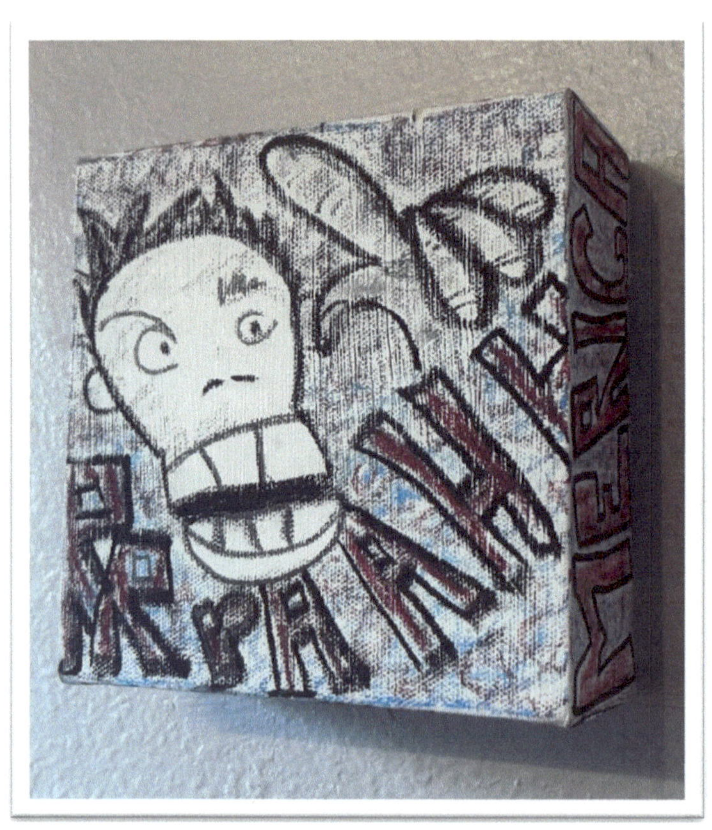

## Judgment Daily

spend life
seeing devils
in strangers
and
alone
reap the fork
the fire
the bitter end

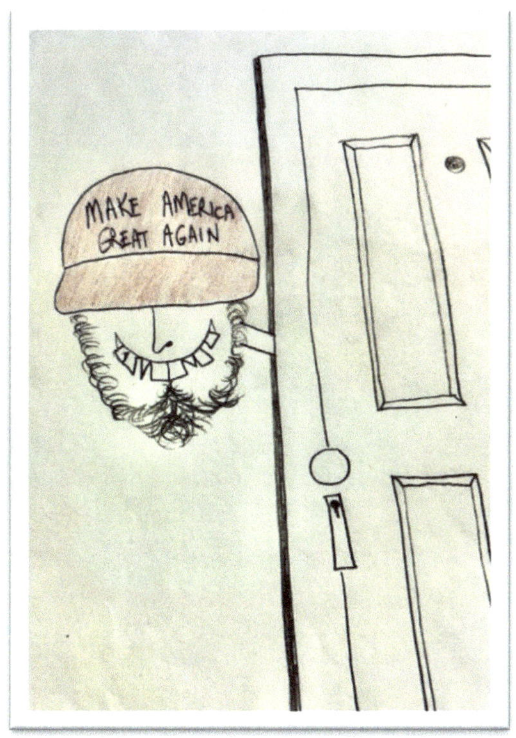

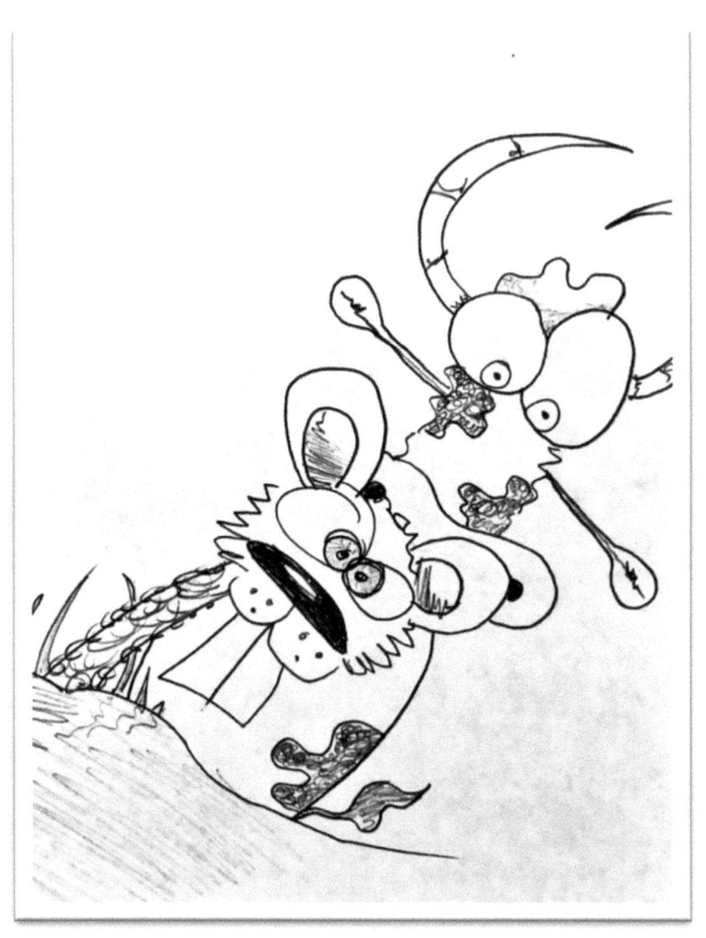

## ALSO BY MICHAEL KLAM

*Emma and the Buddha Frog* (Puna Press)

*The Cheapest Flight to Paradise* (Puna Press)

*Anything for a Dull Moment* (Garden Oak Press)

*Ervas e asfalto* (Ulmeiro)

*Mouthfuls of Red Confetti and the Hunt for God's Skull*:
Miguel Barbosa in translation (Poet's Tree)

*The Square Root of Heaven*: Alberto Blanco in translation
MA thesis, SDSU

*San Diego Poetry Annual* (*SDPA*), associate publisher/editor

*Pozol, SDPA* bilingual edition, co-editor

*Fractal, SDPA* bilingual edition, co-editor

*Imagine, SDPA* bilingual edition, co-editor

*Cantos, SDPA* bilingual edition, co-editor

*Papalotl, SDPA* bilingual edition, co-editor

*Springtime in Paradise* (Border Voices), co-editor

*A Year in Ink,* Volume 6
(Ssn Diego Writers, Ink), co-editor

## About the Author

**Michael Klam** lives with his family in San Diego. He surfs religiously in the morning and sometimes in the afternoon. He spends the rest of the day making weird drawings and writing poetry and staring at one screen or another. He has traveled a lot but mostly loves sitting at home or flopping around at the beach with family and friends.

Michael is the associate publisher of the *San Diego Poetry Annual* (*SDPA*). He co-edits the bilingual edition of the *SDPA* with colleague Olga García. Klam hosts Central Library's *Conversations with Poets,* a series of video and audio interviews, featuring San Diego's finest poets. His publishers are Garden Oak Press and Puna Press.

## About the Book

In this book, the god of fortune gets stuck in the mud, a pink Yōkai refuses to say hello, tragic kittens take pretty pennies from lost and lonely travelers. A father falls behind. A family is found. There is heartbreak and snooze buttons and heroes and villains, and one assassination attempt. The author, too, dies but not really. There are two cemeteries, one goodbye. The multiverse? Irrelevant. There are falcons and tacos, teachers and hissing snakes, banana peels and oil slicks, all things equal and the same. There is love, sure, and seething hatred hatred. What's missing? There is no AI in this book.
There are no rules and no apologies.

## PRAISE FOR *STAY THERE*

Part Japan and Taiwan poetic-travelogue, part musings and drawings, *Stay There* is a thoroughly enjoyable book. Michael Klam's poems exude a playful levity and keen observations on humanity. They have an open-hearted spirit of wonder and surprise, from the importance of knowing how to draw Ponyo, to the "quotient of sorrow," to "a diamond in a drop of anti-freeze"—an entertaining, delightful read.

— LEE HERRICK
California Poet Laureate
author of *In Praise of Late Wonder*

*Stay There* overflows with Michael Klam's signature wit as the poems move through travel observations, familial love, political reflections, memories, confessions, and more. The Table of Contents had me laughing aloud before I even got to the poems! Klam skillfully balances good humor and absurdity with moments of wonder, beauty, and profound contemplation. Reading this book feels like having the best kind of late-night conversation at a pub with a longtime friend. I love it!

— DR. KATIE MANNING
editor-in-chief, *Whale Road Review*

*Stay There* is for anyone who likes their marbles chipped and wayward. This collection is full of surprises, humor, bumps and edges. There are Hot Pot Haikus with full ear chunk corn and skeleton pirate dance parties interspersed with classroom dialogues, practical advice ("Be ready with spoon"), and a visit to a muddy mountain shrine. The illustrations and verse feel organic and unvarnished—like truth spilling out before you can stop yourself.

One of the strengths of *Stay There* is the cohesion between text and visuals. The drawings are as evocative and as rich as the poetry. Both are simultaneously weighty and whimsical. I came away feeling inspired to live boldly — a disposition perhaps best summed up by one word, which is my favorite poem in the book—GUSH!

— **Ying Wu, PhD**
poet, cognitive neuroscientist, UCSD

In these pages, the consonance of voices and visual art leads us to a dazzling, trance-like state where beauty, imagination and daily life converge. Here, the reader will encounter poems as mantras to be nested in mind, heart, and soul.

— **Olga Gutiérrez Galindo**
mathematician, physicist
author of *En el nombre de π* (Ediciones del Lirio y Los Pájaros)

Whimsical and piercingly honest, Klam's *Stay There* journeys through the many meanings of departure and dreams. Moving between sleek trains and smiling bones, these poems ask what it means to leave, to arrive, and to live with joy. Playful sketches and intimate reflections on parenthood bring warmth and unexpected charm to the collection.

— **Daniela Paraguya Sow**
author of *Half Moon Rising* (Kelsay Books: 2024)

Michael Klam's newest collection is cause for delight. Tender love poems, poems of adoration of a father for his children, and the surprise appearance of taco haikus (yes, taco haiku or takus) and so much more all mixed in with illustrations that are fun and sometimes downright silly. I read *Stay There* with a smile on my face, an occasional out loud chuckle, and admiration for this gifted poet and sketch artist. This collection is exactly what the world needs right now.

—JUDY REEVES
author of *A Writer's Book of Days*

In *Stay There,* Michael Klam invites readers into a richly layered world of whimsical sketches and luminous verse. His poems move effortlessly between wit and gravity—at times playful and clever, at others contemplative and piercingly profound. Exploring themes of love, family, travel, and life's quiet revelations, this collection captures the magic found in both the ordinary and the extraordinary. An intoxicating and artfully crafted book that lingers long after the final page.

—JILL G. HALL
author of *On a Sundown Sea*

I am utterly disarmed by these poems. In his unmistakable voice, Michael Klam delivers a book of poems that are humorous, deep, and tender by turns. Did I mention these poems are funny? But that's not all they are. From traveling abroad in Taiwan to eating tacos and hot pot, this book is a feast for the senses. It's also a book with a clear-eyed, abiding love for family. In self-aware family portraits like "The Art-scientific Mandarin Formula of Us," we watch as the Mandarin words for honey, wind and rain, and love—*feng mi, fēngyǔ* and *ai*—are wedded to create the equation for a multi-lingual family. But, just when you think you have this book's visual art and poetry pegged, here comes a mer-cow joke or a memorable image of the Quaker Oats guy with SICKO sharpied on his forehead. So, don't blink. Read. These poems will make you laugh and then move you with their heart-earned wisdom. In his new collection, *Stay There*, poet Michael Klam reminds us that humor slips the serious past our defenses, and we swallow it whole without even noticing.

— CARLY MARIE DEMENTO
editor, poet, literary arts and environmental advocate

Reading this new collection, it feels like I've been visiting with an old friend—but on another part of the globe: East Asia! Fans, old and new, of Michael's work will be reassured to know that his legacy of both informing and entertaining his readers is as laser-focused as ever. Primarily a book of straight-to-the-heart observations, both as foreign traveler as well as local surf-poet guy, these poems let us into the psyche of an oft world-weary man, whose wife and children restore and make whole his humanity. *I would like to remember / how to be in love with the world again* and I know instinctively that he speaks for all of us looking for more than just a little hope in the poetry we consume.

— ROBT O'SULLIVAN
Escondido Arts Partnership

*Stay There* is an eclectic mix of poetry interspersed with whimsical drawings that take us on a journey to Japan and Taiwan, to distant memories of deceased grandparents who seem so familiar, and to places where natural beauty reigns supreme. Michael Klam throws out the rules and throws down a collection that had me laughing one moment and caught in quiet contemplation in others. My favorite pieces revolved around his love for his family. He doesn't just write a love poem for his partner and child; they become the poetry.

— **ALISHA RICHARD**
trans activist, poet, performer

*Stay There* is the book your phone-addicted, passport-clutching, food-obsessed inner voice wants to slip into everyone's DMs. Part travel journal, fever dream, love letter to family and mixed heritage, it says the quiet parts out loud — then keeps going. Klam's musings romp through the life of a retired teacher and dad who's seen enough to be cynical and feels too much to stay there. Self-deprecating, non sequitur, and more comforting than a travel pillow, poems like "Gravity Draws Me Like One of Its French Girls" tenderly serve up social commentary with signature wit. Read this if you'd like to "remember how to be in love with the world again."

— **JANE MUSCHENETZ**
author of *All the Bad Girls Wear Russian Accents*

*Stay There* is a love letter to family.

— **TED WASHINGTON**
artist, poet, editor
author of *Bone Lyre* (Puna Press)

Reading *Stay There, Japan and Taiwan Poems, Visual Art and More,* by Michael Klam, is like having a deep and amusing conversation with a child. This is, of course, a compliment. And a big one! What a gift to be so silly and lucid, so playful and dead serious at once. The sketches of cartoonish animals are a great companion to the poems, adding humor, tenderness, and familiarity. I would say this is a book about journeying and journaling, about living and remembering, about engaging with a world that can speak to us in the form of a deity living in a mountain, a pigeon defecating on your porch, or a horse staring at you. It's also a book about growing old gracefully, meaning without totally adulting, when adulting means to stop marveling at a world so full of beauty that it makes your head and your heart hurt because... beauty does all sorts of stuff.

The poet turns 54, but sometimes he claims to be 65 to get the senior discount. And this is cool but also very alarming, to not stop him from aging even if it's a joke or a lie! The poet is thinking about retirement, he is getting ready for a few *sayonaras,* but also to fall in love with the world again. Indeed, there is so much love, so much hope and gratitude in these poems, that are, nonetheless, cognizant of the horrors taking place in our backyard. Silly poems that turn political while the political turns silly, but also scary and sad. But hope is so stubborn, and everywhere we turn in this book, there is something like a beginning, like the chance to feel "a little less hatred in [our] hearts."

— MARGARITA PINTADO BURGOS
PLNU professor
author of *Ojo en celo / Eye in Heat*

www.ingramcontent.com/pod-product-compliance
Lightning Source LLC
LaVergne TN
LVHW052306100826
845147LV00006B/688